Double Venus

AARON MCCOLLOUGH is the author of one previous poetry collection, *Welkin*, published by Ahsahta Press in 2002, winner of the first annual Sawtooth Prize in Poetry. Aaron McCollough lives in Ann Arbor, Michigan with Suzanne Chapman.

Double Venus

AARON McCOLLOUGH

SALT

PUBLISHED BY SALT PUBLISHING
PO Box 937, Great Wilbraham, Cambridge PDO CB1 5JX United Kingdom
PO Box 202, Applecross, Western Australia 6153

First published 2003

Printed and bound in the United Kingdom by Lightning Source

Typeset in Swift 9.5 / 13

ISBN 1 84471 003 3 paperback

SP

1 3 5 7 9 8 6 4 2

For Suzanne

Contents

Acknowledgments

The author wishes to thank the following journals in which some of these poems first appeared: *The Colorado Review, eratio, Volt, Slope, NC2, Bath House, Word/For Word, Bird Dog.* Thanks are also due to: Susan Wheeler, Lewis Robinson, Matthew Vollmer, Janet and Major McCollough, Donald Revell, Martin Corless-Smith, and Joshua Beckman.

"Certainly no kind of literary learning comes so close to one as does this verdict of conscience: 'You are doing to someone else what you would not like done to you.'"

AUGUSTINE

National Hotel

the city in the poet
is a fact
the city on the island
a fiction

the shadow of the fumes
troubling the air
is a fleeting faction
swimming to the city

"beyond the sport"
and steel and leathern
fixings

touching
the battery and bedsprings
this is the nature
and habit of waiting

or not
daylight

the form of market
dentist   post
collapsible chair

all these locks without
the arguments

bees inside the paper tube
like crickets

I Arguments & Spurious Links

Democrack Pistols

1.

it's all too much   extinguish
the light
of

extinguish

as if a little bit *lex talionis*
as if a little bit Kant & Jesus
        a pinch bat wing   I see
our spells, oh, perfect parking spot inside us

I'm with Gandhi, Western Civilization
        would be a good idea

My main contention: I'm with
Gandhi, Western Civilization would
be a good idea

Let's take a look at that –
                turn the wheel
                visualize the wheel
                nation we turn us
                with determined not to be
                turned

a dirty humanist I'm with us
antipodal
heaven/hell   hell/heaven

2.

"And where weer thow i-bore?" – "I note, I make avowe,
... I axe that of yewe, / For I can tell no more but here I
stond nowe"

3.

perfume in the lining

I a subject in the long
(term) in the singed
horizon as the lids
would throw to "sunshine"

the traipsing gait-styled gate

that gives by organ way*

* that the extra-
physical may be
available to the
eye only in a
very limited
sense and then
only by the
most extreme
good or bad
fortune

the chime of light dements*

* as some
suggest selec-
tion continues

revels   reveals the dig
as just as clearing skies

I-object I brandish
        the angle wing of frame
of window out [*

* even at its
roughest, my
OWN situation

on the future of a wood

        say   the fainting strains

of orphaned hymn
        across the
                waters

coming
turbulence to hand to
better start paddling
    what
we stand on slipping in

4.

... you may joyn
with us in this Work, and so find Peace. Or else, if you
do oppose us, we have peace in our Work, and in declaring
this Report: And you shall be left without excuse ...

... For, the Earth is the Lords, that is, Humans,
who is Lord of the Creation, on every branch of humankind;
for as divers members of our human bodies, make but one body
perfect; so every particular human is but a member or branch
of humankind; and humankind living in the light and
obedience to Reason, the King of righteousness, is thereby made
a fit and compleat Lord of the Creation ...

Tha
t
hed
ge
of
hop
pin
g

littl
e
bird
s
you
hav
e to
star
e to
see

bird no bird no
hedge birds no
head of bird to
no heady   no
bird no bird no

can fall

S
o
yo
u
ev
e
n

c
a
n
se
e
n
ov
e
m
be
r'
s

president *Esau* who if I could forgive him for the
blithe destruction of a numberless train of human
kind would still be nothing to me but a shock that
girls and boys like me were told we could elect as
if a girl or boy could say a word   *tyranny by consent*
                                    a land of younger brothers

floating in the glare of windshield after windshield

        red stage 1
                blue stage 1 and red stage 2

                our patient silent
                        faces in the wash of neon

5.

that dim leveler in which everything
looks the same, everything is
equivalent

      ("at night all cows are grey")

that is not the human life world
we log our grays   lug our grays into
the lights   the light   the floodlight jumping on
and blowing out
                    at night all cows are obstacles
                    that can't be seen
          not the same as trashcans
          behind the house
or deeds and words

there are distinctions even

      obstacles are not all cows that can't be seen

the angel who wants to wrestle
          does anything for a fight

6.

Mencius then said there are no just wars,
but now I wonder now
are there any just terms
for that peace

7.

there have been saints . . .

the burgher saint
                    pouring the silks
             from the window

the tapestry lolling from the
                              ceiling
he pulls   and casts

like the on-treading feet

where man sees his treasure   he says
there shall he also
place his heart (I think, like a cobble)

my heart is for rambling
I mean in my mouth
and the world

8.

Paradise of two coasts   neither near

      (sweet militia rest   or
      when gardens take the towrs,
      and the garrison in   flowrs
               eat garnish)

on this house
      that opens on the street

in the world
      We Ord'nance Plant   and Powder sow

      behind / These trees . . . I . . . gaul its Horsemen
with my interest

in the world   with my speculation

that history is gone   that set of contingencies
we didn't get
      for this set

Therefore have I uttered that I under / stood not;
things too wonderful for me

and look outside
the work of history

the world works on
outside the move of history

and also it does not

[org – *a mild version*]

secret refreshings
    will be done   (thy)
on earth   in this land
I made twelve states in one week
    and saw

doings

        was refreshed

toll plazas springing up
    this is the pike
    CHRISTIAN YOU MUST BE PREPARED

I am
preparing   restless   really on
the road   really   missing home

and in the metempsychosis of talk
    hauling
my wife in darkness and light

she hollows out the melon
        the open secret

    "the first thing a laborer learns is to slow her thoughts
    to the pace of her task, to the speed with which the world
    allows her to move through it," she says

the wealth I count is
    the slow pace of my wife

she/virgil: the task is endless
i/virgil: make good my failure
she/virgil: hard work is the only remedy

but my pace is the 'swifter than dreams' inscribed
      beneath my nation   another flag
                    these colors
           the don't colors   speeding colors
no running by the

     fly my nation and I

swifter than dreams
and the work staying put
          furrowing
          tending

                   how I've been running from it

  every speeding minute

     my wife/virgil: we have covered an immense distance in our
          course

once I keep a hive of bees
          entertaining miniature estate
the skimmed-milk blue boxes
I myself am making   a close framework
entrances narrow   tightly nailed
against extremes
once then I lay out balm and honeywort
       ring the little chime

the angling aiming vortices of their coming

     no (in here) attending to our end
no time in here for thoughts of death

the worker's wiggling abdomen
                      work of dance of

 mortalism
          heresyism

another once I gladly heed instruction   let the mower die

centuries will imminent domain it   came with the house
                                      only runs
                                      without a sparkplug

                    miraculism

and the weeds grow up
and the weeds I savage!

The Anatomy of Melancholy

the trip to Saturn announcement
    this call   (the man in the cab / alone
                            w/ the boutonnière)
    & response   ("the snow falling on the cane fields")

                    AMBITION DESCENDS
to the organs of it and just as early

       the passing jet
       TRANSPIRING

                  ("the hurricane on the pelican butte")
my circle of solitary lectures
worrying pebbles from above

sour stomach   oh I'm swimming there
on pills   bizantium of Michigan

my very self is bizantine   complex of mire and blood
          by the road to the medical complex
          delirious with fear
          traffic light . between . now . and . its remedy

the pedestrian whose sweaty shirt   his joy
knows death will come but leaning into hellish humid blocks
                          hasn't minded

my own invulnerability in him
        raking through the day at furrows   the folds of heaven in

Eyelash

The shouting man is letting out a kite.
The gardeners and the girl spending her day
in the garden breathe from their mouths.
Beneath the phone-booth, the crane, the spout,
circumstance bats again and lets out light.
The girl whispers inaudibly to God,
crushes from her milkweed pod
      the puff of seeds.
Today, the ball of floss remains in sight.
      I go south.
On the edge of it, tangled in the reeds,
I whisper, too, *no insulation.*
To sleep *is* close. But I am not asleep.
Shouting, glaring up, tearing through the leaves.

Apartment terraces face the clay hill.
The tools are bound together with a strap.
I'm falling in with their stone particulars.
The swatch the knot of cloth there on the river
frees itself, is gone. O, breathing girl . . . still.
Still, stay. Sing. In glass or baldechino.
Snapping pennant. To be noble.
      The living grass,
between the stones and through them, wilt.
      The word "curt."
On the tip of my finger: an eyelash.
I can say *enough* again.
The miles of wind, above us, very fast,
light-like, heavy, push, somehow, the miles of mist.

Poem for Jim Thorpe

It was as follows snow which comes upon
itself in round and vigor filling up
this man whose name was english for intrepid
and tracks of elk where they will name a place
for him who killed the last one in that place

There was a sense in trailing like a ring
where two bald fisted men come out and fight
the stripes
of probabilities to save himself
still falling for fear of what's worse than the ground

Whose ground is settled shut up the ground
one did and then another turning white
till men are bound   to slip

Passenger Pigeon

though prim   of little solace (prim though blue)
performing with one wing so "child of man"
what one will call   the wave – the shorter hand
the longer still then suddenly a jewel

to grasp it is   along with fear of death
de facto death   examine wires at night
transecting empty plates of darkling sky
electrified and humming   running west

and into baths of fire on whims of fur
forever crossing arms against the ledge
the sweat of such an accent   only sweat

or one who would not   for who can   rather
what hopes remain but civil hopes – engaged
I hope   I can believe   I bend to sit

Firing the Arrow

The steal along with the discovery.
Also lapses.
The fire, shelter, flurry of wing and neck –
the hatch, the snow – the flying in snow.
The not flying. Nutcracker clickers go quiet.

Burrowing things: a seed in river glass.
For hours, I've been simmering lentils
to leave her guessing.
Apply. Or, gather kindling for the route.
The fingernails unpeel, and peels right you.

The mountain story drawing its own shape.

Tried tried. Now another may begin.
The plastic pipe that frames the bottom shelf.
I have dry matches.

However the rocket goes, I go there.
I lighten myself. I lighten the symphony.
Had companionship:
clock and bridge. My love is waiting.
Destiny and faith and greens in the sink.

The roof was grass and gone in the candle.
Our metal from caches.
So God could see, I said, and tore together.
This just fell into the pot. This safe.
Another day of glints, culets, and cards.
Bleeding and bleeding, right, bleeding into it.

Memoranda (cc: Self and Soul)

All hail the kind, the kind man is dead
        , my kinsman,
(or I've touched the red twelvemo
        and buried it).

As the busy to bib, who cut and molded
notches in his late magnificence – soaked
– silked – with open neck and flowing cuffs,
Am I
        in doing what I was made to

                        |You, face to god's manifold, unzip
                                and water the daffodil

As the partita ends, the third critique begins
with fragile crosiers piquing the bridge
between the waters and the waters
        is

        it

        good

                        |does it walk through the streets with a
                                                mirror

It does walk through the streets
degaussing them all that hoot their toy horns
        and exalting them tamely
til bringing their comely heads down

– behind me the man is pointing his finger
the woman beside him –

they're gone. Is he pointing
at gossamer
                        |he's chastising the leaf for the fall
                              the brass, mould, and spurious
                                                    livelihood
                        an article sent abroad filled with
                                                    whiggery
                              blasted by winter, wedded to
                                                    hyacinth.

Here I am wood within this wood:
the ghost of my father's father blowing the dust
                        from the robin.

Song for John Wesley

forgetting lyrics here and there the vault
with peeling paint and bealing chips of voice
that is the studio   where god is voice
only   entrusted to the line the caulk

the flexible seam collecting response
if dust then dusty circuit   pulse riding
at overwhelming moments fixing eyes
on the wall   *hosannah*   fragrant fragment

"arise my soul arise and shake" for god
the voice in the voice   the wholly other
analogized in feeling   human sing

the open chamber is the special body
in the world of things   arise my father
and mother of song   my human being

They Are as They Are

~~At mesmer~~   into palette
the good world wavering
between titmouse and a word
for it   *passim* the little
birds are clogging up my gutters

the polar thing composite in the
world
         the bear on hind legs
hugging at his project

         in perpetuity   stuffed *passim*

happy/sad is the world
                    is nature

is being contingent on the poem

so the motive of
the step-widener (animal in quotations)

what might spill over
or waver out

in the value-added way

watch the seam for signs of wear
recover *passim*

poll the auditorium

assaying (a saying) with the eyes

the dialectic green on

the smart eyed   inarticulate creature

II   Common Places

Common Places

As good a place to start
~~where all~~ where all mornings start
shut in and quiet
the common ground of good
will I share with others
the floor I share with her
(unlock the door my love
our feet on it again
on earth again our earth

Suzanne (as an object)
asleep
              a lump of comforter
awake
              a handsome yawning girl

beautiful society!

Fyrst arise erly
Serve thy God deuly
And the warld
besylly

in line of sight   in line
through breaks in the screen
to mean
a thing
to be

in babylon-and-zion-one or the track not
a metaphor for the bear but the bear
a metaphor for the track

you should have seen the host
you *had* to see the host

but I am walking in
the day   reflected in
the windows   making plans

the snow is waving off
the walk   hard and soot
adrift   the drift)   my plan:
believe what heat I feel
is sent from space to ME

an say-us-na sairlie,
but sauf us frae the ill-ane

worried so much about
the state of in   I'm worrying
the hardwood floor between
my wife and me three feet
the body of our soul
together back to back
at work at worrying

the body of our soul
together
                a work of worry

It is better to marry
to marry

to marry is
not
not to burn

to marry not
to burn
is to burn in

counterfeit gloom

every switch being thrown
the draft beneath the door
the light beneath the floor   (I left on laundering)
this cozy little work of persisting

are you breathing   enough
as good a place
                         to start

III Essays and Visions

[log – *a mild vision*]

1.0 – himself

that's okay   letting go some bees today
the old man kept in slatted wooden crates
obtaining to the husbandry of bees –
a bluish white in places where the paint
has been repainted (the new color
skimmed milk as one dips rags in kerosene
at an impasse) – and expecting the worst

triggering some smoke then running behind
the rusty boiler
                    to admit confusion
as a wedge (the wedge we have is painted
a flaking red, misshapen at the face)

            must admit not knowing what to do
                            and so confusion

the soul has had enough   meaning
        the wait
            the genius of this place is "was":
the same rose blows . . . nothing changed but the hives

            and this is america!
. . . the bees stealing out and in . . .

1.1 – *walt*

that's okay, wedge   and over here, sleepy
with the humming of the bees / with industry /
admit a tablet to prevent confusion
then proceed   proceed
proceed with hacking at the privet root

the task at hand: planting twenty hemlocks
measuring the room between and burying
the soily bulbs   evergreens over years
they grow and overgrow
                         and they are like your bees

1.0 – *himself*

then i will sing to make the work feel swift
my love is less afraid   at night i sleep
and less and less afraid   i may yet come
to love the world beyond my bed   beyond
                                    my love

1.2 – *a rube*

eros by any

the same rose blows

can't do better than that

than   a toast

a toast to thanatos?

1.3 – *w.c. bryant & (a rube)*

the solemn brood   (what of such love?)
of care plod on   (where learned?)
and each one as before   (to what may love be girded?)
will chase his favorite phantom

1.0 – *himself*

(remember what to let) some letting go
the privet lies unhedged, and we're
defenseless so between the hedges   and okay

she has come to work
and I have come to work

shall I describe her precision against my berserk:
      with a piece of fruit
          the roots
          the

and she loves to rest   my love is precise

if the day is full of troops
               returning
the day is full of fear

where all must move their homes
                    with which fear
we comply and move

1.4 – *his will & his love:*

> *evry will desires purity w/o turba int   powr xtends*
> > *holds in subjexion*
> *(less it escape fromt)   therefore the weak doth run and*
> > *seek the limit,*
> *hidden in mystery, sought by all creatures*

love: not confused but out of control. good:
     to labor is not to love: though loving
     and leave the weeds   no ugliness in plantain
     nor beauty in grass   don't dare distinguish
     the green from the green   not sisyphus flower
     from narcissus from wandering jew

will sings of devices and a positive love:
                posits a love:

Essay 1. A Day of Rest

Selah, the empty mess hall blown through   winds stronger when there is rain – it may be the rain pushes the wind; or, the rain may be captured by such great winds from some other place and carried here.

A catalog of raptures from the reeking creosote: this man wears a jacket; the buttons are shell; does his passivity make his jacket less than his cape or shawl; there are three visible pockets which may now contain and/or conceal anything small enough to fit them. Submerged to the eyes in his bathtub – he closes his hands and sputters drawing handfuls of water (which undulates). This problem with his breathing.

Wooden rectangles found on inland waters are something else; or, the water on which they're found – some room, though nearly invisible, opens between for some force like wind or breath.

The hall's high frames – within triangles – manage to hold the roof open to the place below the wizened fig. The bolts pock; continue their work of rusting. The swifts keep the floor from smoothing out. Lighting on a beam, the swifts shadowed. The triangles: perches. Frames holding perches up. But regard the silhouette of a bird or of a small flock together at rest. A feather's tip upsides in wind.

Essay 2. A Day of Rest

In gauging the look of the idiot, the community turns to an atoll, saying (and so on) we admit it. A petroglyph on the boulder derives a line resisting: man and woman should stand up straight with one eye.

~

we were crushed

~

The rain is a depth chart of orders and ordeals; beautiful but not obsessed: obsessed but not so gray. Into the dripping leaves and slicker, the paramour (name "splintered dawn"). Inveigling translation and, with a breath, translator. The parapluie droops from her shoulder, and the money tree only looks dehydrated.

Essay 3. A Day of Rest.

[A] To a daisy, silvering, lacing the hillocks' turns, river going to the battery. Half cloth, making love [B] with a marker she's placing between pages. In her fingers. The sort confounded in a corner [A] with cursive bands of tangerine after squatting to pee – the ivy wavers in and out and dries in the shade. The bundle of twigs and limbs falling from their loop-drawn strap; who knows how long we'll tramp them underfoot:
> *Versamur ibidem, atque insumus usque;*
> *Atque in se sua per vestigial volvitur annus.*
Solitude and panting alike in the pocket of vines – adventitious rootlets adhere to the stone and the bark without [C] penetrating anything.[1] [A] But we count on shade and sun, distilling our water in a tattered can.

Hirsute to the wrists and ankles, I am [B] no longer a child storming the glassed-in bird houses. We're both looking up in the pattern of geese from white towards newer densities. [A] And back down dispersing ants from onyx. Not, as a boy I had wanted, to lay a hand on anything in violence. Watching my foot.

---

[1] *'oo; stopping – in this may be a natural hierarchy.* But . . .

Essay 4. A Day of Rest

It's cinnabar mid-leaf and limply shadowing diminutive shapes: the tree in a round of shell blasts   staggering beasts   fragments of beauty. This one plumbago except where it's sheered reflective   torn into a dun trunk. Those communards doing again in the names of isthmus' contested: *we hold this animal paris* (the blood everywhere – the length of their forearms, on their trousers, beading and smearing on planks of town square as they pivot and shake) *to be the transparencies of triumph.*

Essay 5. A Day of Rest

Plow plow plow from the contractor. Even-pitched but strident, from no form remarkable but voice. Concrete and lawns so far rendered: the former sprinkled with various pebbles, the latter crabbed here with wide-faced leaves there with sunburn. These acres all alive and ~~ordered~~ half-commanded. Eaves, fence posts: silhouettes of these and other missiles. The man with his injury hovers between – seeding; reeking; caked with the marks of kisses.

Trickster Hermeneutics

on the road to damascus   met the indigenous
person, damascus, [mystic indios   atoms of god] a bird.
The image of: honor (molting   so some bald) : temporary
(color of the hat in the high sun) : determined (the scaly
legs, neck)
         s/he speaks: "for all the
     walkers pedate
        the fliers cum turtle cum
declining day

of: the war, "who but an industrialized patriarch would think
that winter can be vanquished"

   : the petals on the tree
like past the spirit voices   the 23rd highway
and past that detroit beginning

s/he before (the petals on the tree)
had been speaking
     that I lost voice   changing voice
     by phone
     punching two for more

s/he host   mother and father of
endings and confidence
             the glare and free
                society

lag between covenants runs
the jagged way to damascus
     "for that reason s/he lengthen out
the buckle cord of us life
and cause the golden moment to move on . . .

. . . the crow full of figs saying how do you
spell 'ah hah'"

or the minority (for human being)
"separated from the multitude by a peculiar lot"

Time One

position in the tune

I here   the doges that look us in the eie

beside the piles   so that I am changing

put the hand on the leafing floor and wet

the doges alarums

inside of history   believing in righteous

devices (the shape of space to dynamic justice:

read agnes heller

> (6) The incomplete ethico-political concept of justice does not
> design, propose or conjecture any particular social system as
> *the* good or *the* just one. It presupposes that there may be
> several good or just systems, each quite different in nature.
> For all possible laws, rules and socio-political norms and
> rules are good and just by definition, if they are legitimized
> by all concerned in a rational value discourse, under the
> guidance of the universal maxim of dynamic justice, at the
> time of legislation.

forest acrostics   sea caves   I here   wind

in the leaves of the density   keening for a reason

between the wood and the water

walking on dirt   the angels are speechless

the angels are there and not there   here

the broken engines   heaps

the walls of tune

Stanza

PURPLE — spaces between the chips of limestone cover this and
we swim

      in the, now flooded with

SAPPHIRE (the color of a good death), quarry.

                        HIDDEN PURPLE (the color of
                             automatic* death) they
paint the pennants.

*that is, attended by procession

      what sped flywheel; what governed timing belt; shut off
      caution red and yelling out in the street that doesn't
touch

                    like a box
           in illustration-like   filled with the
           real valuable

      storm cloud   as said   this color
                       lifting pieces up across the
                               ~~ghost of~~
                       habit wearing up and down

humankind people,
light in,
consider *me-you* in the silurian tan of
the Eternall God, who am UNIVERSAL Love, / and whose service
is perfect freedome, and pure Libertin- / isme.   "mechanism
that distinguishes and unifies *at the same time*."

no automat   no autonomic
at hand as ever
in arms
when arms

      this [   ] is for not the globe,
&c.

Stanza

no telling   abroad
                                                       at home
                                                       though man,   man
                                                         with fountain pen

I can say that I got it

the   street   in   the   next   to   the   street
                    and the other and other in sight

from the mountain in my mountainous city
        the city
                    the network of hashes

on the street in my university town
        the man turns corner and is gone

form folds into essence

                there is essence   the French burn it in their
        deux chevaux

MATERIUM − the color of mail routes

on the pavement of
        string

                        astringent of
                        rain

        the ants emerging from this shadow of
me and the gas nozzle
                the shadows of heat dispersing to heaven, &c.

Stanza

all the way up to the building BREAKING CLOUD – this sidewalk
this rough
    cotton of the work coat or soft of hooded sweatshirt

gusty corners and storms of flyers (this one color AGRARIA*

        I am injured by
        sitting by and letting
  the huron

           goose in   color   punts contrary to the
                            current dragging at
                            punting

     I anticipate
on my feet

           propelled into the ditch by the ditch
                 dug around
            GREEN IS OR

"grow the rushes"   in the lull

I implore*
   *beating plowshares into plowshares

        And hatz the penaunce apert of the point of myn egge,

by this mark's instruction: the instrument panel (c) fits snugly
                                      into
place and disappears, &c.

---

* beating swords into plowshares, pacing the gravel gardens of towers
blades of grass dunning the brick walk

[62]

Blues Matrix :: War Time

go moses, I lend to the service: head.
I can't let my feelings as the compound
hand-made standing in for the latin
to call from space the ants of the earth
            bear on this   so I love humankind
    disgusting   and fail to
as someone else might say to mark himself:
the child is blond and white and empty
            empty in the air and brutality
the temperate day we say is in
our nation – our American nation
that hides a heaven, yes   that switches
sources   that is the train car   where the
southern crosses the dog

Shipwreck of the Singular

1.

geese, ducks, swans   the tall grass called
maiden hair grass

and   right
                    against the headline

            detroit police sick and tired
                    of finding dead babies

our "at this point the
discussion becomes academic"
way of rising

in Gallup park   not feeding
the water fowl   who stay here but a term

we go on paving stones

night unseasonably cool for Tennessee
in Michigan and Canada   dry air
across the bed

this is our new home   we are lying down

2.

it was delivered thus

the road that runs in front of home is fast
buses and cool gliding pedestrians
making noise en route to another road

heaven is a beautiful

I once   (once I
        was straight

head   on   shoulders

        had headed

had the ones

        ballad hunter   balladeer

dear, if you want to get to heaven on time
lord knows you got to [   ]

I know

I know to feeling until feeling no longer
    need to know

beautiful place ————— there's hundreds of daylilies

    not just orange but tiger huntress carnelian and crazywork

and the cake-type mountain described is a real
with some of the friends who tried, or a little at last

not bitching about the work   they reek
they roll the giant shopping carts through ruts

deep gravel   not-so-shallow fords

once*   nothing but a thing

*I once had

still quite hot —— sure, and up hill except for some scenic vistas
one called needle head

the ground falls away
                    further

            the scene: some more of the friends
            building a sandy starter ramp

the way is zooming iodine
                but slow

        the seeings a jaundicey

fog-bound

                and virgo's hands again

"she tried to arrange for a trip
   over to the island, where the people live
   in very primitive style and sing tunes that
   go back to slavery and earlier times. But
   transportation for our machine-was- and
   the heavy batteries needed for supplying
   the power was a problem that we did not so
   ,as only row-boats were available. Another snag:"

AND THEY SHALL BE CONFOUNDED

I do not know

but one   I one   through the vents in my head
heaven [scratch]

earth = the origin of metaphysical belief
b/c earth is a wilderness of labor

another snag

                    sang the sirens between two roads

and came the furies to shit
upon our solemnity this night

we let it slide

so long S'wanee
I learned a lot upon the mountain (beat)

not that

heaven is a beautiful place

lord knows you got to [   ]

I come back to the geography of it
                    the sandstone bands
                    Cumberland Plateau

in lieu of that beneath my feet   I don't know
                    cushion of conifers like nails in a pail

and their faces

3.

of being numinous, G. Oppen and the addition

my mother and father of birds   I saw an angel @ the CN tower
that is, I looked @ the CN tower in Toronto, Ontario, Canada
        August 23, 2001

Here Magi – Here! The young woman is

hearing the voices raising receipts and

rubber bands

rejecting one for another for a false compass

    Jeremiah: This captivity is long

            build houses   dwell in them   plant gardens

            eat fruit   take wives

            increase

            seek peace   have peace

            I   gather   countries

            will   they   be   safely   brought

            gate   of   the   self   fall

O my mountain in the field
my pleasant portion

my mother and father of birds   it is not in man that walketh to
direct his steps / correct me, but with judgment; not in thine
anger, lest thou bring me to nothing

I would adjust my friend's terms; say *gardener* "your handiwork
                                                  stops and starts"

4.

but we *are* a government
    me, mine, numerous others' others

and we are sick   we are all sick

and tired

of death   even as we long for heaven
    "Oh that my head were waters" – Jerim.
    "I have pictured it by a river/Secret to America
    but wholly American" – DR

what about this "spanging" (a student taught me this)
wretched polis   relief for America's workers printed right
on the check I cashed and spent on making mirth

this was no relief but
    "this shall seem, as partly 'tis, their own" – Sicinius

that partly 'tis

behind the daydream   the day   that wholly is

"every man that is mad / maketh himself a profit"   we
walk (my mother, my father, my wife)
the perennials @ the Canadian Royal Gardens

5.

there is the rock

there is the honey

in the rock there is honey

even if the honey looks like grains of sand

even then besides the grains

honey

               "sung in the dreaming voice of
the sponger"

               like unto the amber in the second sight

the choirs of angels in the rock in the sea

not the rock made to look like the rose
not the resemblance in the rock

      the rose in the rock

a list of some who're seeing it: D., B., K., W., W., O., Z., J., R.

honey defined as honey, which is made by bees, in the rock

6.

this
disordered
spring
late summer this
swarming
with caterpillars
        flowers
choked up
        fruit trees
all unpruned
        hedges
not ruined

I would make a little comedy
even under   in the compass of
        a pale

        dangling apricocks   bending twigs
        sprays   weeds
                wholesome flowers

by way of just walking
"in the 'yellow spot' of clear vision"

we at time of year / do wound the bark, the skin
of our fruit trees, / lest being overproud in sap and
blood / with too much riches it confound itself

I would make a comedy

knowing   prison   unto
               unto world unto

I in one person many people, / and none contented; sometimes

        with nothing shall be pleased,
till he be eased / with being nothing

        FULL OF DAYS, AMEN

comedies   de vegetabilibus
comedies   de animalibus
        of earth, air, and leaf

wherein one's humble weeds are weeds
        and free
                but not dead
sick and tired of finding dead
        a pitiless world

IV Double Venus

[(0.38+0.333i) *ecumenon*]

season feather
with the sumac still sweet

beginning (over fruits of the valleys
   crease
                 worked dark
and by crookhand
            smudged dark in the night walk
are
   there candle covers
  in the fell there nails and burrs
accounting stars of the metropolis
         in the cloud

    bringing wild berries from the fringes
of the wood of the hairs of the berries

    journey barefoot)

   to rain
in my state   in this filling over season

[(0.27+0.57i) *american man and woman, election year*]

we
as water or mercury moves from its whole
from the cusp of something
words without our having to
                    quote

there   have been   saints

and we   *are more disposed to suffer, while evils are sufferable*

are legion in our delight
deep and pending in every single drop

[(0.39+0.22i) *a hero and a patriot*]

terrifically wounded   the poisoned cape
and the river   javelin to the amazon

our bird hupping between dumpsters
by sharping and
robbing, he is generally poor   lousy

loving generalities
the honey of a world of nothing but sound
    with the right foot of baked clay
        resting more on this

brass ball   brass talons
  scaled brass leg
          read by

the clear-cut   with enormous equipment

Resistance in the Materials

The girders save from nothing   holding up
from nothing nothing   (more today of frets)
children in coffee   my issueless cup
and all need extra-strength   the concrete sets

the people stand around the puddling pee
devouring pastry flakes   on earth to make
is tangled   the spirit is consuming
it swells inside and rises like a cake

the oven cake and self: self cake   call hell
its on my mind   *my very self a hell*
the birthday party boots it not   to hell

thirty-one years   a friend to god but not
an asset   drilling holes in air but not
a girder   living paradise but not

[(-0.62+0.43i) *jack spicer*]

called for bitter weeds . . .
"the talcum milk or
      "a question in the raising
dispelled by the burying ground

I (my better) dresses down
      swiftly passing
scenery   I (I)

if there were no continentals / allowing
    us to move along
        as in the emblem: pills & soap
their conversation in natural
light borrowed down with
a paper ticket,

if cold blooded were the judgment
and floating the
    assize,
  in would lessen in

[(0.28+0.54i) *trustee*]

myself: I am with K
on the roof of the unfinished
mansion
looking at the stars

I can't say what I see
     except being here
more than what I see

the invisible trail behind me

          (all that's mine in the old sense
          the mangling prescience)

newer sense   now   myself
with K

the darkness of the house below
          awaiting its balconies

[(-0.36+0.62i) *raymond williams*]

another woodcut
    stained

          broken cornered

    chestnut

the pauper's portable   the pauper's block
                    running my fingers across shal-
low   deep   and shallow-deep   on pocks   and ridges

and see   as far
    as miles of fishes beyond the silt

    picking at it
    drummed from the work of picking

        flaws

Coffee County Breakdown

to shake my savior's hands and hands and shake
my savior's hands
this stutter eyed drive   pied ponies   peonies   poems
      satellite dishes to shake my savior's hands
who called   my christian name and swooping shadow
big enough to snatch my little dog to dark
                              in the field where I am stung
by sweat-bees   good for them that stinging is their lot
      and stinging are they

I am shaking in my hands
                              around the cabin in the chair

so I
can sing
I'm made
to shake
the song
vibrates
                  like water at the dam in latin
            could make a fountain of

      is said to

[(-0.62+0.43i) *nomas*]

overheater   open water
where sun is pendulum like seeing as
        seeing is pendulum like sun

                of the circling shadows
                man of
                of the man of

water the sharp of cold   as if cutting or burning (re: genius of
                                                            feeling)
        the man of "feelings": *when not of this humor I am of another*

not ingenious not disingenuous – a spring from a rock

                to
                a gully and flash over in ribbons

the rest and the rest of the sun
                so I am in my senses   turning

in the water breaking   the water curling back
        the rest of the string

[(-0.72+0.35i) *sunday morning, facing westward*]

in god in front of home the bird I know
not   -now in god   -now seeing the bird make
the sound I think a hoot   but not the owl
what this and this bird make is not music
so why make music   -now the hoot with cree
-now

because I'm here to hear and see god
  say god and nothing know not even
              names
of birds or Iandgodandbird   one word
         against the unassailability

Line Changes

is a piece of pie the sun rising in the gorge a piece of the plate

    not what is meant by this happening
    some use this glass for the drinking of gin

cheers to the cheerful spring   the water spilling away from
the cold first report

    not put to use
    this is what it is or craziness

[(-1.03-0.34i) *in the swash*]

guffaws – a window

the flake
of paint
in tapping
in the wind
against one sash bar proves

(the osprey landingcry
above a nest, the tall
alarm, a rotting tree)

we have
no strength to.

a leg   we're down and horizontal   O
singing are our eyes, o, seeing

[(xx+xxi) williams island]

its dorsal effigy   (it's bound and wet

the   back   of   plate

                    geometries   the dome

Chiaha / Fuller : "(2) the metaphysical universe embraces
            the physical—both being finite, for the metaphysical
            is mathematically demonstrable as being always
            one tetrahedron greater than any physical system;"

        – a turtle in stone

rising to island   force to give not get

                        and flexion in the water's force to shine
unheavy   sitting prints of earth on earth   I am awake for

floating and sinking

[(-0.12+0.74i) *anathanthema*]

the island   is land
but not   a land

NOT   THE
NOT   A

This   demi paradise

   s   emi   ar
                    i
               d

           parad   e

by the river curculio

the canis river

    a s

     is

thick and

full of red fabric

Lefthanded of Blooming Late

lefthanded of blooming late
   in this paradise

reading   mor nin g's

                 riot

    omnipotent has mismeant
and we inhabitants

may   tend to

the blasted polar pansies
    wrinkled in the frost

the lefthand
          fo(u)ndling

daffodil or iris

shoot

 never knowing subtlety
greeting whatever paradise
    may be

Romanticism

A gavel of rain browns down the stored up
like cockney john unclipping the values
*the vowels – cork-polished glass green from the nub –
removing himself, removing his shoes.
"Cough" just the spelling of it: oh you gee
aitch: diagnoses the spell and the spin
to the room just a jitter on the sea.
Garden magic I am mumbling again.
So, not on the sea but the barber's house
cupping my neighbor my brother myself
with better magic bullhorn better voice.
Got gravely in the river to health.
I welcome the atoms as he does:
removing the kerchief's transistors.

Rhyme (Occident)

orange skin of orange

I bought an orange

continuous

world

is what ear heard

Eagle Mountain Breakdown

for the gregarious but tending in the lips
towards drought
    might say arroyo with a smile for sewer

and I guano or droppings for shit

but shit is fine and so all rivers flow to the shitty sea (also fine)

the breeze is unseasonable   the dark is early
the edge of the cliff is right there

    where before all this dark there was valley to mountain
    there is holler and holler back (oh, and the lights of town)

unlike the stars of number

[(-0.5+0.56i) *chang ming, july 1999*]

the dogwood blooms blew
hung in the wind
that   thank god   in that heat
  setting out from the house
with no sleep   no food

what was I reading   in the world
how bearing on
  the blossoming

    that I
changed
  by which I was changed
momently
 enough to see   world
 in the world
 in my own
that I
image
  hung

[(-0.52-0.57i) *summer: silhouette & continuum*]

the kingfishers   about how they (the birds?)
nest on their own rejectamenta

some stand around the derelict moorings
with heads of feathers' pointings'

        they turn to some sky and some to us
        on the sand in the boat on the low lagoon

 Sis and I   K and I   Suz and I   floating like
                                              we are in our bodies in
                                              regarding

in a ball / of oneself / is a buoyancy